Picture the Past
Life in
New France

Jennifer Blizin Gillis

Heinemann Library
Chicago, Illinois

Produced for Heinemann Library by
   Bender Richardson White.
Editor: Lionel Bender
Designer and Media Conversion: Ben White
Picture Researcher: Cathy Stastny
Production Controller: Kim Richardson

07 06 05 04 03
10 9 8 7 6 5 4 3 2 1

Printed and bound by Lake Book Manufacturing, Inc.

Library of Congress Cataloging-in-Publication Data.
Gillis, Jennifer Blizin, 1950-
   Life in New France / Jennifer Blizin Gillis.
      p. cm. -- (Picture the past)
Summary: An overview of everyday life from 1639-1760 in New France, an area which included parts of Prince Edward Island, Nova Scotia, New Brunswick, and Quebec, as well as parts of several states in what is now the United States. Includes bibliographical references (p.) and index.
   ISBN 1-4034-3799-8 -- ISBN 1-4034-4286-X (pbk.)
   1. Canada--History--To 1763 (New France)--Juvenile literature. 2. New France--Social life and customs--Juvenile literature. 3. Canada--Social life and customs--17th century--Juvenile literature. 4. Canada--Social life and customs--18th century--Juvenile literature. (1. Canada--History--To 1763 (New France) 2. New France--Social life and customs. 3. Canada--Social life and customs--17th century. 4. Canada--Social life and customs--18th century.)
I. Title. II. Series.
   F1030.G47 2003
   971.01'6--dc21
                              2003005403

Special thanks to Angela McHaney Brown at Heinemann Library for editorial and design guidance and direction.

Acknowledgments
The producers and publishers are grateful to the following for permission to reproduce copyright material:
Canadian Museum of Civilization, Hull, Quebec, p. 22. Corbis Images/Nik Wheeler, p. 30. Fashion book, Paris, 1875, p. 8. Malak Photographs Limited, Ottawa, Canada, p. 24. North Wind Pictures, pp. 1, 14, 20, 21, 23. The Bridgeman Art Library: Archives Charmet, pp. 9, 19; British Library, London, U.K., p. 6, 15; Christie's Images, London, U.K., p. 7; Lauros/Giraudon, pp. 17, 18, 26; National Gallery of Art, Washington, D.C., U.S.A., p. 12; National Gallery of Canada, Ottawa, Ontario, Canada, p. 25; Private collections, cover and pp. 3, 16, 29; Royal Geographical Society, London, U.K., p. 11; The Stapleton Collection, p. 10.

Illustrations: Mark Bergin, p. 28; James Field, p. 13; John James, pp. 4, 27.
Map by Stefan Chabluk.

Every effort has been made to contact copyright holders of any material reproduced in this book. Omissions will be rectified in subsequent printings if notice is given to the publisher.

ABOUT THIS BOOK

This book tells about the daily life of people in New France from 1639 to 1760. New France was made up of three colonies in North America: Canada, Acadia, and Louisiana. The **colonies** were founded by the European country of France, starting in the early 1660s. This book deals mainly with the colony of Canada, which was the area of land around the St. Lawrence River Valley. Its three biggest towns were Quebec, Montreal, and Three Rivers.

We have illustrated the book with paintings and drawings from colonial times and with artists' ideas of how things looked then.

The Author
Jennifer Blizin Gillis is an editor and author of nonfiction books and poetry for children. She graduated with a B.A. from Guilford College with a degree in French Literature and Art History. She has taught foreign language and social studies at middle schools in North Carolina, Virginia, and Illinois.

Note to the Reader
Some words are shown in bold, **like this.** You can find out what they mean by looking in the glossary.

CONTENTS

New France

In the 1500s, French explorers began coming to North America. Some were looking for gold and jewels. Others were looking for a way to get to the Pacific Ocean in order to reach Asia by ship. The first explorers were not interested in staying in North America. Later, explorers began to claim land and start forts. Little by little, much of North America was controlled by the French. Some was controlled by **Great Britain** and Spain. New France stayed French until 1760, when the British took over most of the region.

Look for these
The illustration of a New France boy and girl shows you the subject of each double-page story in the book.

The illustration of a trapper and canoe marks boxes with interesting facts about life in New France.

TIMELINE OF EVENTS IN NEW FRANCE, 1639–1760

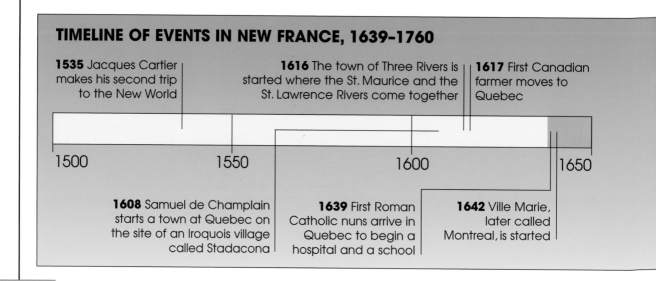

1535 Jacques Cartier makes his second trip to the New World

1616 The town of Three Rivers is started where the St. Maurice and the St. Lawrence Rivers come together

1617 First Canadian farmer moves to Quebec

1500   1550   1600   1650

1608 Samuel de Champlain starts a town at Quebec on the site of an Iroquois village called Stadacona

1639 First Roman Catholic nuns arrive in Quebec to begin a hospital and a school

1642 Ville Marie, later called Montreal, is started

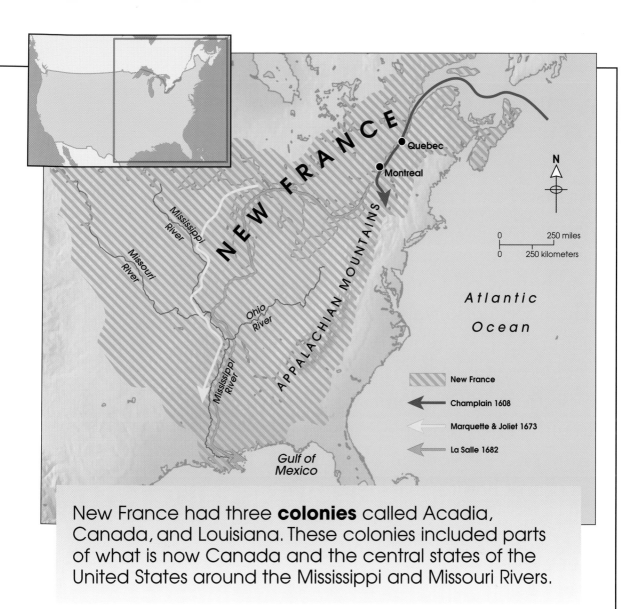

New France had three **colonies** called Acadia, Canada, and Louisiana. These colonies included parts of what is now Canada and the central states of the United States around the Mississippi and Missouri Rivers.

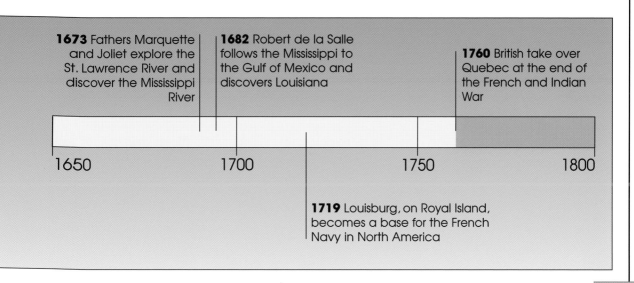

1673 Fathers Marquette and Joliet explore the St. Lawrence River and discover the Mississippi River

1682 Robert de la Salle follows the Mississippi to the Gulf of Mexico and discovers Louisiana

1760 British take over Quebec at the end of the French and Indian War

1650   1700   1750   1800

1719 Louisburg, on Royal Island, becomes a base for the French Navy in North America

A Harsh Land

At first, New France grew slowly. Not many people wanted to go to this part of North America. Winters were long and bitterly cold. Summers were hot. There were also wars with the Iroquois going on. The French government decided to make it easier for people to settle in their **colonies.** They gave wealthy French people, called lords, large pieces of land in New France. By law, lords had to give land to anyone who asked for it. So, some people were able to trade crops for land.

French explorer Jacques Cartier explored the area around the St. Lawrence River and claimed it for France. This 1536 map shows a small drawing of Cartier exploring the area that would later become Canada.

This painting shows a winter scene in Canada in the 1700s. A horse pulls a sleigh across the snow and ice. Winters were so harsh that soldiers who were ordered to go to Canada wanted to return to France as soon as they could.

The people who farmed the land were called **habitants**. Because winters were harsh, they had a hard time making things grow. But life was still better than it was in France. In New France, habitants only had to give a little of what they grew to the lord. They could keep what was left over to feed their families, or they could sell it to make extra money.

PLEASE COME!

In the 1600s, most people thought New France was a "frozen desert." Popular writers, who had never been to New France, wrote about winters that lasted for eight months and land covered in snow and ice.

Servants and Wives

Many of the people who first went to New France were soldiers or men looking for work. Men who could not pay for the trip went as **indentured servants**. They had to promise to work for three years for a family or a community. In return, they were given a place to live and food to eat. After three years, the indentured servants could get land and become **habitants**, but few wanted to stay. Those who wanted to return to France were often given a free journey back.

A few criminals were sent to New France as a punishment. There they could slowly work their way to freedom.

The French king realized that if New France was going to be successful, people needed a good reason to stay there. He saw a way to convince men to settle down in New France. In the mid-1600s, he began to send "King's Daughters" to New France. These were not really his children, but young women whose parents had died or who were poor. They were expected to marry and stay in New France to raise a family.

When hunting in winter, habitants wore snowshoes.

KING'S DAUGHTERS

When a King's Daughter signed up, she was paid 10 French pounds of gold. That was about the same as the yearly salary of a **craftsperson.** Just before she left France, she was given these things, too:
- 30 pounds for new clothes
- 60 pounds to pay for her trip
- a money box
- a hood to wear in winter
- a head scarf to wear in summer
- 100 sewing needles
- 1,000 pins
- a comb
- white thread
- a pair of stockings
- a pair of gloves
- a pair of scissors
- two knives
- a bonnet
- food for her trip

Jobs in New France

In the larger towns of Quebec and Montreal, there were wealthy merchants and people who worked in the government of New France. Many **craftspeople** lived there, too.

In France, it took a long time for someone to become a craftsperson. Then, he or she was allowed to do only one kind of work. But in New France, craftspeople often did many kinds of work. For example, a person who made cloth might also make hats and clothing.

Three fur traders are shown here, trading with Native Americans. On their journeys, fur traders slept on the ground. They used their canoes as a kind of tent. They ate dried corn, peas, or pumpkin mixed with any meat or fruit they could get along the way.

TRADE GOODS

Instead of money, fur traders paid the Native Americans with trade goods. Certain things were worth a certain number of pelts. The most popular trade goods were knife blades, axes, cooking pots, socks, blankets, and colored cloth.

Traveling through Canada was often very difficult. If rivers were too fast or too deep, canoes, supplies, and goods had to be lifted from the water. They were carried over land to the next river.

Most of the fur in France came from New France. Many Canadians became fur traders. The most popular fur was beaver, because it was used in making hats. Traders spent many months traveling to the far north to get **pelts** from the Native Americans. To get there, they traveled in large canoes like those that Native Americans used.

11

Native Americans

Native Americans in Canada were Eastern Woodlands peoples called the Algonquin and Iroquois. The Algonquin were hunters who moved from place to place. The Iroquois stayed in farms and villages.

The French settlers thought the Native Americans were intelligent and wise. If settlers wanted to criticize the French government, they sometimes wrote letters pretending they were Native Americans.

DIFFERENT LOOKS

Many French men in the 1600s had blue eyes and pale skin. Most Native Americans had darker skin, dark eyes, and dark hair. When they first saw the French men, they were shocked at the way they looked and made fun of them.

Some **settlers** in New France wanted to farm on Iroquois land. Here, a French settler tries to make a deal with the Iroquois.

Fur traders spent a great deal of time with Native Americans. Many of them married Native American women. Most French settlers were **Roman Catholics,** a Christian **religion.** By law, if a Native American agreed to become a Roman Catholic, he or she could have the same rights as a French settler. Many groups of Native Americans did **convert.**

Many Iroquois lived in longhouses. They cut poles from young trees, tied them together with vines, and covered them with tree bark. Several families lived in each longhouse. The Iroquois built a tall wooden fence around the group of longhouses to protect the village from enemies.

Life in the Country

The first **settlers** in Canada lived in fort-like villages called habitations. **Habitants** built their houses to look like the ones they had left behind in France. Most homes were made of wood, but some were built of stone. Later, some were built on stone **foundations**, which were filled with mud and straw to make them warmer. Homes were heated with fireplaces. Habitants had to cut and store enough firewood to last through the long, cold winters.

FRENCH SUPPLIES

Habitants made most of what they needed. Things they could not make were brought in from France. These included pots, salt, blankets, hats, gowns, shoes, socks, weapons, and nails.

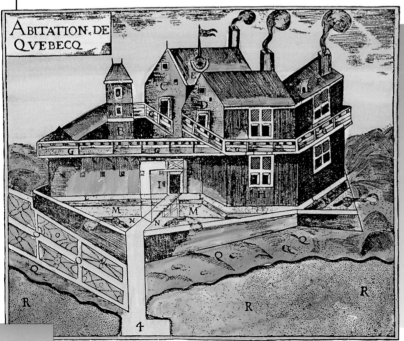

ABITATION. DE QVEBECQ

Habitations were built in the style of Champlain's fort in Quebec, shown here. They were surrounded by walls that soldiers guarded. As Canada became more settled, people started to farm outside the shelter of the walls.

Wealthy people built homes made of stone. Churches—like the one shown here—were also built of stone. Most buildings were made to look like those the habitants knew from France.

For habitants, barns were almost more important than houses. Farm animals could not live outside in the Canadian winter, so barns had to be large enough to hold all of a farmer's animals and their food. The roofs of barns and houses were very steep, so that snow would slide off instead of piling up. Roofs were made of tiles, shingles, or wooden boards.

Life in Town

Quebec was the **capital,** or main town, of the **colony** of Canada. It was divided into two parts that were separated by a long stairway. Wealthy people lived and worked in the upper town. **Craftspeople** lived and worked in the lower town.

Ships coming from France sailed into the port, which was in the lower part of town, as seen here. Near the port was the main square and cathedral.

QUEBEC

A. Le Fort
B. les Recollets
C. La plate forme
D. Les Jesuittes
E. La Cathedralle
F. Le Seminaire
G. l'Hostel Dieu
H. L'évêché
I. La Redoute
K. Le magasin apoudre

In towns, the main streets were wide. This is a view of Rue des Recollets, a main street in the center of Quebec. On the right, a group of soldiers march along the street. In the center of the street, townspeople stand and talk.

Houses and businesses in Quebec were crowded together. If a fire broke out, it would spread quickly. Laws were passed to protect the town from fires. Houses had to have tile roofs to keep them from catching fire. Brick or stone walls separated each building from the one next to it.

People had to clean out their chimneys every two months, and they had to pay a **tax** on each chimney on their house. The tax money was spent on leather buckets, which were used to carry water if a fire broke out.

Religious Life

The **Roman Catholic** Church and the French government worked together to build New France. The church wanted **priests** and **nuns** to go to New France to **convert** Native Americans to the Roman Catholic **religion**.

French leaders of the Roman Catholic Church were not always welcomed by the Native Americans.

Roman Catholic priests who have sailed from France arrive in Canada. They will learn Native American languages and try to spread their religion to the Native Americans.

The town of Montreal was started as a **mission,** which gradually grew into a large city. Nuns started schools and hospitals, hoping that many Native Americans would come to the towns. They started poorhouses, too. These were places where poor people could live and get free food.

Native Americans did not want to live in the towns. Soon, priests began to live, work, and travel with Native American groups. They did this to learn the Native American languages, and to try to encourage the Native Americans to convert.

THE GIVEN

Priests often had to travel long distances from the towns to reach groups of Native Americans. They sometimes left a "given man" with the Native Americans. These men were not priests but ordinary Roman Catholics who agreed to stay with a group of Native Americans and show them how to live a religious life.

Clothes

Wealthy townspeople wore the same clothes that rich people wore in France. Men's and women's clothes were made of silk, velvet, or wool and trimmed with lace or embroidery. All the clothes were made by hand. Women wore caps or bonnets, and men wore fur hats.

Wealthy people wanted to look their best. But clothes from France were expensive. Wealthy people sometimes bought less food to save the money for buying clothes.

TASSELED CAPS

Most habitants and fur traders wore long, cone-shaped, stocking caps called *tuques* (TOOKS). Tuques were knit from wool yarn and had a wool or fur tassel at the tip. Because the caps were handmade, each one was different.

In the country, **habitants** made their own clothes. They used wool or cloth made from plant fibers, such as cotton and linen. Woolen clothes were warmer and worn mostly in winter. The habitants copied some of the clothes that Native Americans wore, such as mittens and moccasins made from animal skin. They often lined their hats and coats with fur.

Habitants gathered at village dances. The men wore shirts, knee-length pants, and stockings on the legs. The women wore shirts, lace-up jackets, and long skirts. In this scene, behind the dancers in the center is a **nun** wearing a head-covering and gown.

Home Life

In the country, **habitants**' daily lives centered around their farms. But in the evenings, people often visited each other's homes. They played cards or board games and sang songs.

On the first day of May each year, habitants had big May Day parties. These were all-day celebrations. They would decorate a tree with streamers, have a feast, and dance.

Habitants cooked food, dined, and relaxed in the main room of their farmhouses. Everyone in the family had to help with farm chores, such as chopping wood for the fire, feeding the animals, and, in winter, clearing snow from the front of the house.

In large towns such as Quebec and Montreal, wealthy people visited each other's homes, too. They held concerts and dances or played cards. They also took long rides in their carriages and went hunting or canoeing. There were also formal dances at the governor's palace in Quebec.

Native Americans were often invited to join celebrations and feasts. During the long, cold winter, social events were very important occasions.

GALET

Galet was a very popular game in New France. A galet looked like a round, flat pebble. The game was played on a special table with a long, straight groove carved at both ends. Players tried to slide the galet from one end of the table to the other without it landing in the groove.

Children and School

Schools in New France were run by **priests** or **nuns.** Children usually started going to school when they were about eleven years old. Most children only stayed in school for a few months or a year at the longest.

If a boy did well at school, he might go on to study to become a priest. Girls and boys who did poorly in school were sometimes sent to a trade school, where they learned to become servants.

The **Roman Catholic** Church set up colleges, like this one in Quebec, to train priests and nuns to become teachers. In schools, they taught children French, science, geography, mathematics, and **religion.**

Wealthy families often hired a friend of the family, known as a governess, to care for their children. She would also teach the children good manners.

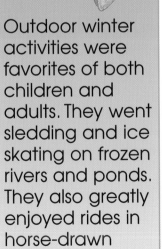

WINTER FUN

Outdoor winter activities were favorites of both children and adults. They went sledding and ice skating on frozen rivers and ponds. They also greatly enjoyed rides in horse-drawn sleighs.

In schoolrooms, children sat on long benches without backs. There were a few tables and a stand where the teacher stood. Teachers carefully guarded their school supplies, because they were all sent from France. There was only one book for reading, so children took turns reading from it. Only the teacher was allowed to touch the book or turn the pages.

Food

Habitants grew corn, peas, pumpkins, wheat, oats, and beans. They hunted animals such as deer and pigeons and fished for salmon, cod, and eels. They also ate a lot of pork and beef. The most basic food habitants ate was bread, because it was easy to make and store.

Cooking pots and pans and other kitchen equipment, such as those in this painting from about 1620, were brought over from France.

New France Recipe—Maple Sugar Candy

Many maple trees grew in Canada. Native Americans showed the first French **settlers** how to make syrup from maple tree sap. They used maple syrup to sweeten many foods. Settlers often made maple sugar candy and served it as a treat at winter parties. They usually made this candy by drizzling the syrup over snow.

WARNING: Do not cook anything unless there is an adult to help you. Always ask an adult to help you cook at the stove and to handle hot liquids.

YOU WILL NEED
- 1 heavy pot, such as cast iron
- 1 candy thermometer
- 1 large cooking spoon
- 1 cookie sheet coated with cooking oil or spray
- 1 cup (240 ml) maple syrup

FOLLOW THE STEPS
1. Heat the maple syrup in the pot over medium heat until it reaches 280 degrees F (138 degrees C).
2. Use a spoon to drizzle shapes of maple syrup onto the cookie sheet.
3. Put the shapes in a cool place to harden before eating. Store them in a cookie jar to keep them fresh.

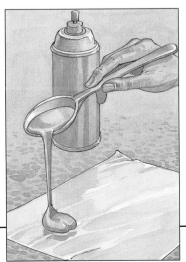

Britain Attacks

As soon as the French began their **colonies** in New France, the British began to attack them. For more than 100 years, parts of New France went back and forth between France and **Great Britain.** For a long time, the French were able to keep New France for themselves.

In the French and Indian war, many Native Americans helped the French fight against the British. But the Iroquois helped the "Redcoats"— the British soldiers.

In the mid-1700s, Great Britain and France began to fight the **French and Indian War.** Both countries wanted to control all of North America, but Great Britain had more money and a stronger army. First, the French lost Acadia, the part of New France that was on the Atlantic Ocean, to the British. Then, British troops took over Quebec and Montreal. In 1763, Great Britain won all of North America east of the Mississippi River.

The French thought the British would not be able to attack Quebec because it sat high on a hill. They thought they would be able to shoot at the big British ships as they sailed slowly up the St. Lawrence River. But this old painting shows how the British sneaked their soldiers into Quebec in small boats.

New France Today

Today, Canada stretches from the Atlantic Ocean in the east to the Pacific Ocean in the west. Quebec is the only **province** that is still French. The **capital,** also called Quebec, is the oldest walled city in North America. Visitors can still walk on the walls and tour many buildings and shops in the old city. French is the official language of the province, but many people there speak English as well.

Today, the city of Quebec is mix of historic buildings and modern offices and apartments. What began as a tiny village is now a large city with a port, government headquarters, and busy streets.

Glossary

capital city where the government is located

Christian religion based on the teachings of Jesus Christ

colony small town created by people from a different country

convert to change from one religion to another

craftsperson someone who makes something for a living, such as jewelry, furniture, or pottery

French and Indian War war that was fought by French and Native Americans against the British

foundation bottom part of a house that holds up the rest

Great Britain country formed in 1707 by England, Scotland, and Wales. The country is also called Britain and the people are called British.

habitant settler in New France who was given land to farm in exchange for giving some of the crops to a landowner

mission place where people live, work, and pray together

nun in some religions, a woman who never marries and gives her life to helping the religious community

pelt fur of animals such as beavers, foxes, and rabbits

priest in certain religions, someone who leads religious services and performs ceremonies

province a section of a country that has its own government

religion system of belief in God or gods

Roman Catholic belonging to the religion whose leader is the Pope

settler person who makes a home in a new place

tax money that must be paid to the government

More Books to Read

Ansary, Mir Tamim. *Eastern Woodlands Indians.* Chicago: Heinemann Library, 2001.

An older reader can help you with these books:

Harmon, Daniel. *The French Exploration of North America.* Broomall, Penn.: Mason Crest, 2002.

Sherman, Josepha. *Samuel de Champlain.* New York: Rosen, 2003.

Index